NOW YOU CAN READ....
DAVID AND JONATHAN

STORY RETOLD BY ELAINE IFE

ILLUSTRATED BY GEORGE FRYER

Library of Congress Cataloging in Publication Data

Ife, Elaine, 1955-
    David and Jonathan.

    (Now you can read—Bible stories)
    Summary: Recounts the shepherd boy's relationships
with King Saul and Jonathan and the way he became king
of Israel.
    1. David, King of Israel—Juvenile literature.
2. Jonathan (Biblical character)—Juvenile literature.
3. Bible O.T.—Biography—Juvenile literature.
4. Bible stories, English—O.T. Samuel. [I. David,
King of Israel. 2. Jonathan (Biblical character)
3. Bible stories—O.T.] I. Fryer, George, ill. II. Title.
III. Series.
BS580.D3I343   1983   222'.409505   83-13820
ISBN 0-86625-219-3

Published by Rourke Publications, Inc. P.O. Box 868,
Windermere, Florida 32786. Copyright © 1983 by Rourke
Publications, Inc. All copyrights reserved. No part of this
book may be reproduced in any form without written per-
mission from the publisher. Printed in the United States of
America.
    The Publishers acknowledge permission from Brimax
Books for the use of the name "Now You Can Read" and
"Large Type For First Readers" which identify Brimax Now
You Can Read series.

GROLIER ENTERPRISES CORP.

NOW YOU CAN READ....
DAVID AND JONATHAN

David was a young shepherd boy. His father had eight sons and he was the youngest. The older boys became soldiers in the king's army. David was left at home to look after the sheep.

One day, a stranger named Samuel
came to David's home. He told
David that God had chosen David to
be a king when he was older.
David was surprised, but he did not
say anything.

Some time later, David was taken to
see the king of the country who
was King Saul. David was very good
at playing the harp. King Saul
liked to listen to him play. He
asked David to stay at the palace
with him.

David was a gentle boy and a brave one too. Once, a great giant named Goliath, came with his army against King Saul. No one dared to face the giant, but with God's help, David stood up to him. He killed Goliath with a stone thrown from his sling. King Saul made David a leader in his army.

When the army came home after the battle, people came out of their houses. They danced and sang in the streets. Everyone was happy. The people loved David. Everyone said how brave he had been. King Saul was very angry. He was afraid the people would make David king in his place.

From that time, whenever King Saul saw David, he became angry.

One day, the King threw a spear at David to pin him to the wall. David ran from the room. David became very unhappy living at the palace. He became afraid of King Saul.

Jonathan, the King's son, was kind. He was a good friend to David. They made a promise to each other that, what-ever happened, they would always be friends.

"I can see you are not happy here," said Jonathan. "You must leave the palace. Take my armor, my sword and my bow, in case you need them."

David did not go. He did not think that he was in real danger.

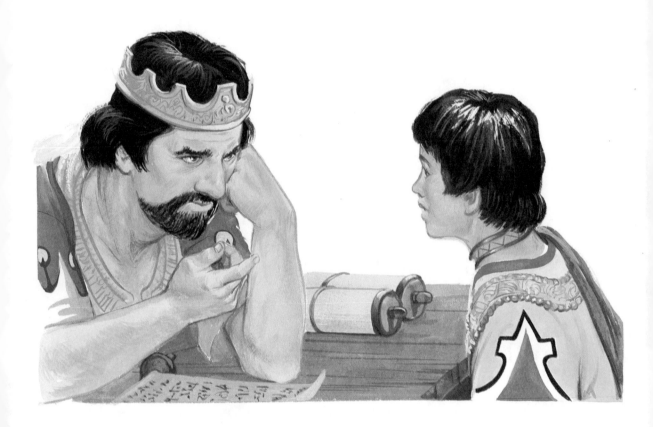

King Saul came to hate David. He told Jonathan to kill him.
Jonathan loved David and so he made a plan.

"In a field not far from here, there is a great stone," said Jonathan. "Go and hide behind it. In three days, I will come with my servant and shoot three arrows by its side. If I say to my servant, 'Go and find the arrows, they are beside the great stone,' then you will know that all is well. But, if I say, 'Find the arrows, they are ahead of you,' then you will know that there is great danger. You must go away."

So David hid behind the great
stone. Jonathan went to King Saul.
He begged him not to kill David.
King Saul did not listen. He
became very angry. He threw his
sword at Jonathan, but it missed
him.

Jonathan ran from the palace, calling his servant. He went to the field near the great stone. Soon his arrows flew through the air.

"Find the arrows,"
called Jonathan.
"They are ahead
of you!"

David heard and he was very sad.
The servant found the arrows.
Jonathan sent him home.

Then David came out of his hiding place. He put his arms around Jonathan.

"My father is so angry. I am sure he plans to kill you. You must go away," said Jonathan. "Hide far away from here. You must remember our promise. We shall always be friends."

David ran away. He found a cave near the desert, where he lived for a long time.

Other men who were afraid of King Saul joined David. When he was older, he became their leader.

One day, someone asked to see David.

It was Jonathan. A long time had passed. Jonathan hardly knew him. They threw their arms around each other.

"You need not b afraid," said Jonathan. "My father will never find you. One day, you will be king and I shall serve you. Until then, we must part."

Jonathan went back to join his father's army.

Some years later, David heard that there had been a great battle. One day, a soldier from King Saul's camp came to David. His clothes were torn. David could see that he had been in the fighting. He told David that King Saul and Jonathan were dead. He brought the King's crown with him. He gave it to David.

David wept. He was very, very sad. God had made him a king, but David had lost his best and dearest friend.

All these appear in the pages of the story. Can you find them?

Jonathan

Goliath

David

King Saul

arrows

the great stone

crown

cave

Now tell the story in your own words.